Planets

Uranus

Dash!
LEVELED READERS
An Imprint of Abdo Zoom • abdobooks.com

3

Level 1 – Beginning
Short and simple sentences with familiar words or patterns for children who are beginning to understand how letters and sounds go together.

Level 2 – Emerging
Longer words and sentences with more complex language patterns for readers who are practicing common words and letter sounds.

Level 3 – Transitional
More developed language and vocabulary for readers who are becoming more independent.

abdobooks.com

Published by Abdo Zoom, a division of ABDO, PO Box 398166, Minneapolis, Minnesota 55439.
Copyright © 2019 by Abdo Consulting Group, Inc. International copyrights reserved in all countries.
No part of this book may be reproduced in any form without written permission from the publisher.
Dash!™ is a trademark and logo of Abdo Zoom.

Printed in the United States of America, North Mankato, Minnesota.
092018
012019

Photo Credits: iStock, NASA, Science Source, Shutterstock
Production Contributors: Kenny Abdo, Jennie Forsberg, Grace Hansen, John Hansen
Design Contributors: Dorothy Toth, Neil Klinepier

Library of Congress Control Number: 2018946204

Publisher's Cataloging in Publication Data

Names: Murray, Julie, author.
Title: Uranus / by Julie Murray.
Description: Minneapolis, Minnesota : Abdo Zoom, 2019 | Series: Planets |
    Includes online resources and index.
Identifiers: ISBN 9781532125324 (lib. bdg.) | ISBN 9781641856775 (pbk.) |
    ISBN 9781532126345 (ebook) | ISBN 9781532126857 (Read-to-me ebook)
Subjects: LCSH: Uranus (Planet)--Juvenile literature. | Solar system--Juvenile
    literature. | Planets--Juvenile literature.
Classification: DDC 523.47--dc23

Table of Contents

Uranus 4

Many Moons 14

Studying Uranus 16

More Facts 22

Glossary 23

Index 24

Online Resources 24

Uranus

Sun

Mercury

Earth

Venus

Uranus is the seventh planet from the sun. It is the third largest planet. Scientists have discovered 13 rings that surround Uranus.

Uranus has no solid surface. Its **atmosphere** consists of hydrogen, helium, and methane. The middle of the planet is an icy slush of liquid and gases. The core consists of rock and ice.

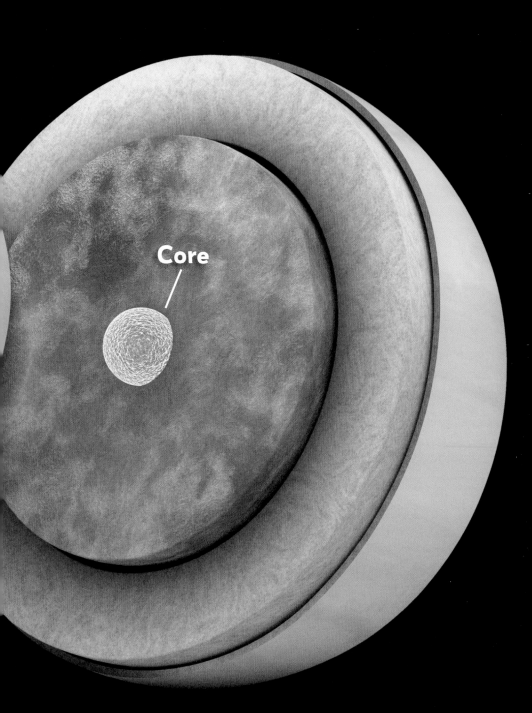

Core

Uranus would not be a fun place to live. Its average temperature is -357 °F (-216 °C). Winds on the planet can reach more than 500 mph (804 kph)!

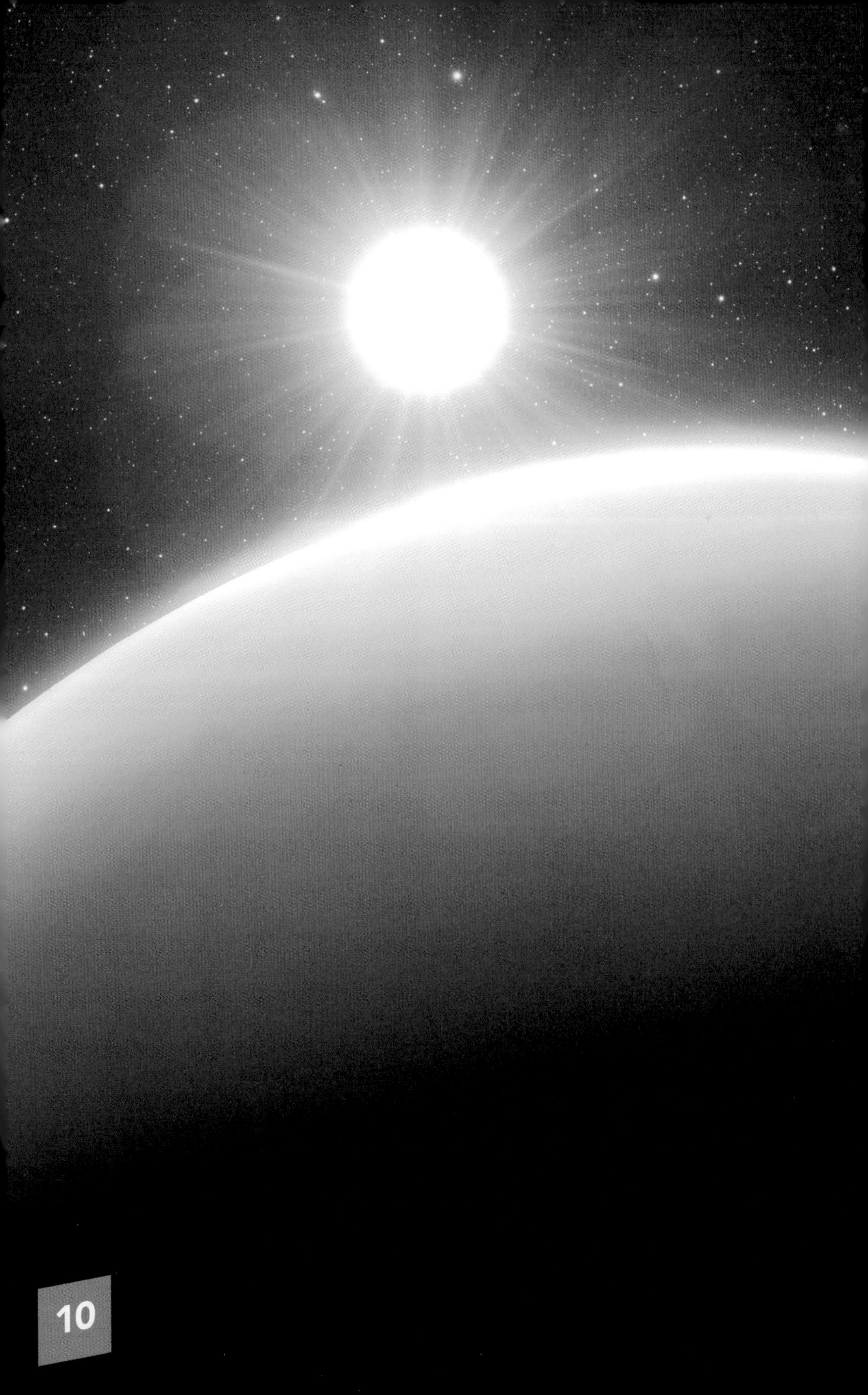

It takes Uranus 84 Earth years to **orbit** the sun one time. It spins as it orbits. It takes 17 hours and 14 minutes to complete one rotation. This time is equal to one day on Uranus.

Uranus is unique because it **orbits** the sun on its side. Its spin **axis** sits at a 98° angle. Long ago, many large objects may have collided with the planet and tipped it on its side.

13

Many Moons

Uranus has 27 known moons. Titania is the largest moon. The moon Miranda has canyons that are 12 times deeper than the Grand Canyon!

Studying Uranus

Voyager 2 visited Uranus in 1986. It discovered 10 smaller moons. It also learned that many of the planet's rings were made up of rocks, dust, and ice.

In 2017, the **Hubble Space Telescope** spotted two bands of light, called auroras, on Uranus. They are caused by powerful bursts of solar wind that travel from the sun to Uranus.

The Keck telescopes are located on top of Mauna Kea mountain in Hawaii. They have provided the best look at Uranus. The telescopes observe the planet's seasons, rings, and moons.

More Facts

- Uranus is 1.8 billion miles (2.9 billion km) from the sun. It takes about 2 hours and 40 minutes for the sun's light to reach the planet.

- Uranus' 27 known moons are named after characters in William Shakespeare's plays. Bianca, Puck, Cupid, and Juliet are a few of them.

- People first thought Uranus was a star. Sir William Herschel later deemed it a planet after observations in 1781.

Glossary

atmosphere – the gases surrounding the earth or other planets in our solar system.

axis – a real or imaginary line through the center of an object, around which the object turns.

Hubble Space Telescope – built by NASA and launched into Earth orbit in 1990. It observes and takes photographs, and transmits the information back to Earth.

orbit – a curved path in which a planet, or other space object, moves in a circle around another body.

Index

atmosphere 6

composition 6

day 11

Hawaii 20

Hubble Space
    Telescope 19

Keck telescopes 20

Miranda (moon) 15

missions 16

moons 15, 16, 20

rings 5, 16, 20

sun 5, 11, 12

temperature 8

Titania (moon) 15

weather 8

year 11

Online Resources

Booklinks
NONFICTION NETWORK
FREE! ONLINE NONFICTION RESOURCES

To learn more about Uranus, please visit **abdobooklinks.com**. These links are routinely monitored and updated to provide the most current information available.